MW01168950

The AUTOBIOGRAPHY Of *Al-Muḥaddith* Muqbil bin Hādī al-Wādiʿī (رَحِمَهُ ٱللَّٰهُ)

Translated by Abū al-Ḥasan Mālik al-Akhḍar

Ibn al-Akhdar Publishing

Second Edition: 1446 AH/2025 CE
Originally published by Al-Rahmaniyyah Press, now a subsidiary of Ibn al-Akhdar Publishing House.
ISBN: 979-8-89940-527-3
PO Box 8671 Turnersville, NJ 08012 U.S.A.
Electronic mail: editor@ibnakhdar.com

Cover Art by Ibn Al-Akhdar Publishing

"To me, reading the *Ṣaḥīḥayn* [of al-Bukhārī and Muslim] is the sweetest pleasure in the world. When I open al-Bukhārī and read, ''Abd Allāh ibn Yūsuf narrated to us: Mālik narrated to us...' or see *Imām* Muslim say, 'Yaḥyá ibn Yaḥyá narrated to us...' I forget all the worries of the *dunya* and its problems."

—*Al-Imām* Muqbil, *Al-Ṣaḥīḥ al-Musnad*

Table of Contents

Translator's Foreword

"WHERE IS Mālik?" the *Shaykh* called out. I was sitting near the middle of the *muṣallá* among hundreds of other students in the *Ṣaḥīḥ al-Bukhārī* class after *'Asr*. I raised my hand.

"I'm here, O *Shaykh*."

"Stand!" he said.

I put down my notebook and stood up preparing myself for the *Shaykh's* question. He paused for a moment and smiled.

"How many narrators named Wakī' are mentioned in *Taqrīb al-Tahdhīb*?"

I thought hard but could only recall one name. "Wakī' ibn al-Jarrah," I said and looked up.

"Is he alone?" he said.

I shook my head, uncertain.

"There are three: Wakī' ibn al-Jarrāḥ, Wakī' ibn 'Udus, and Wakī' ibn Muḥriz. Sit!" he said.

The benefits of this teaching method—questions and answers—are widely known, and anyone even remotely familiar with our *Shaykh* knows this was his way. He would constantly quiz the students, and not only during the lessons. Whether sitting at lunch, walking through the *wādī* (valley), or standing by the road, the *Shaykh* would question those he encountered on almost any subject: *ḥadīth, 'ilm al-rijāl* (the names and lineages of narrators), fiqh, *ʿaqīdah*, Arabic language, history, etc. This is just one example of the *Shaykh's* adherence to the Sunnah, for this was also the teaching etiquette of Allah's Messenger (ﷺ).

Al-ʿAllāmah Muḥammad b. Ṣāliḥ al-ʿUthaymīn mentioned that the Prophet (ﷺ) used this method to gain the listener's attention and to make him ponder the question carefully. It also helps to fix the answer firmly in the respondent's mind. Nearly eighteen years later, I still remember that there are three people named Wakīʾ in *Taqrīb al-Tahdhīb.* (Several years after I left Dammāj, the *Shaykh* asked me another question. One whose answer I have not forgotten either.)

I was informed that our *Shaykh* was in California receiving treatment for a liver ailment. So, I traveled to see him. When I entered his hospital room, after greeting him, I said in Arabic, "May Allah heal you completely, O *Shaykh.*"

"Ameen," he replied. He asked, "What is that supplication's *ʿIrāb* (grammatical inflection)?" Knowledge was most important to our *Shaykh* and remained his focus even during his sickness.

RECENTLY, I was invited to give a series of lectures on the life of our *Shaykh* in Pittsburgh, PA. I thought reading to the students from his autobiography would be beneficial, as I remembered how it strengthened my resolve to seek knowledge many years ago. I hoped that hearing the

Shaykh's experience—in his own words—would have the same profound effect on the listeners as it had on me.

In this book, the *Shaykh* chronicles his tribe's history, his first efforts to seek knowledge, his travels to the Kingdom of Saudi Arabia—where he studied in the Islamic University of Madinah and sat with some of the great scholars of the day—and, finally, his homecoming to Dammāj to establish his *masjid* and center. From that center, *Dār al-Ḥadīth*, the *Salafī* call would spread to every region of his land, and beyond.

This short, moving account is a brilliant introduction to the life of the noble scholar of Islām, the *Muḥaddith* of Yemen, our *Shaykh*, Abū ʿAbd al-Raḥmān, Muqbil b. Hādī al-Wādiʿī. I pray to Allah that it benefits and inspires all who read it. May Allah have mercy on its author and grant him the highest reaches of Paradise.

Written by one in need of his Lord's pardon,

Abū al-Ḥasan Mālik al-Akhḍar

28th of *Ṣafr* 1438 *Hijrī*
Camden, NJ USA

THE AUTOBIOGRAPHY

THIS LETTER IS FROM Muqbil b. Hādī b. Wādiʿī to his brother in faith, *al-Shaykh, al-ʿAllāmah*, the noble historian, the beloved Muḥammad b. ʿAlī al-Kūʾ.

Al-Salām alaykum wa Raḥmatullah wa Barakātuhu.

After sending salutations, I welcome you and your dear letter. By Allah, several people have requested that [I pen my life story], but I declined because I have many preoccupations. Also, I dislike publicizing such things. However, *Shaykh* Muḥammad, whose discourse is sweeter than honey, has a place in my heart, so I could not refuse him.

I am from Wādiʾah, which lies east of Saʿdah, near the valley of Dammāj. You—may Allah preserve you—described this valley in one of your commentaries, I believe in *Ṣifat Jazīrat al-ʿArab*, with clear detail about its gardens, trees, and plants. Perhaps Allah will make it easy for you to visit the students of knowledge in Dammāj, and you will see, Allah willing, what pleases you.

I am Muqbil b. Hādī b. Muqbil b. Qā'idah al-Hamdānī, al-Wādiʿī, al-Khallālī, from the tribe of Ālī Rāshid. Our elders say that Wādiʾah is from Bakīl.[1] However, you, may Allah preserve you, know more about genealogy than me and others, as this is your field of study in which none of the contemporary [scholars] rival you.

The Wādiʿah Tribe

THE Wādiʿah can be found throughout the different regions of Yemen, but most of them, as far as I know, live in Saʿdah[2]. They reside in Dammāj, to the east of Saʿdah, and in Saḥwah[3] above Dammāj beneath Mount Barāsh, al-Darb, Āli Hajjaj, and al-Tulūl, which lie between the eastern and southern parts of Saʿdah. North of Saʿdah, they dwell in al-Zūr, Āli Na'il, and Āli Riṭās, and al-Razamāt, in the valley of Nushūr[4], and in Ḥāshid, west of al-Sanʿāniyyah'. The Wādiʿah are called "Ḥāshid" because they live in the land of Ḥāshid.

There are Wādiʿah living in Najrān, in the upper part of the Najrān Valley, and others in Ẓahrān to the south. One year, a group of our tribesmen passed through *al-Qarārah* Center, north of Ẓahrān, and when they handed their passports over to the authorities there, they called out their names. The officers said, "Whoever is Wādiʿī, stand to the side." So they did so and said to themselves, "What do they want from us?" When [the authorities] finished calling out the names, the soldiers shook their hands and said, "We are from the Wādiʿah of Ẓahrān, and you are our guests. We must host you." So, they promised to visit them upon their return from *Hajj*, Allah willing. On their way back, they visited them, and [the Wādiʿah of Ẓahrān] hosted them with the utmost generosity. They longed to meet the Wādiʿah of Saʿdah, the tribe's main lineage.

The Wādiʿah, like many other Yemenī tribes, lacked proper religious instruction. Still, about forty of their youths regularly attend the lessons. We will mention some of them, Allah willing, in the list of students.

I praise Allah, for most of the *Wādi'ah* who live next to Sa'dah defend me and the *da'wah*. Some defend the Religion, and some protect me out of tribal loyalty. If not for Allah—and then for them—the enemies of the *da'wah*, especially the Shi'ites, would not have allowed any trace of us to remain.

I recall some of [my tribe's] stances and ask Allah to reward them with good. One time, I faced harsh opposition in al-Hādi Mosque for turning people away from the Shi'ite call there. The men of Wādi'ah and others stood by me and rescued me. The Shi'ites desired to do away with me. This was during the presidency of Ibrāhīm al-Ḥamdī[5]. The evil ones from the communists and the Shi'ites raised their heads, and they imprisoned me for eleven days during the month of Ramaḍān. Some nights in prison, around fifty youths would visit me. Other nights, about one hundred and fifty men from the Wādi'ah would come to the authorities, pressuring them, until they finally released us. All praise is for Allah.

Also, when the enemies of the *Salafī da'wah* would sometimes come to Dammāj armed, but the people of Dammāj would drive them out in disgrace.

Another example is during travel. If I said, "We wish to go," they would compete—may Allah preserve them—to accompany and guard me. On some trips, we traveled in as many as fifteen vehicles.

In those days, the *da'wah* was was in its best condition. I praise Allah because I had grown older—nearly sixty-two years of age. The experiences and advice from those who love the *daʿwah* led me to be gentle and avoid engaging with enemies who offer nothing but curses and insults.

﴿ خُذِ ٱلْعَفْوَ وَأْمُرْ بِٱلْعُرْفِ وَأَعْرِضْ عَنِ ٱلْجَٰهِلِينَ ١٩٩ ﴾

> "Show forgiveness, enjoin what is good, and turn away from the foolish (i.e. don't punish them)" [*al-ʿArāf* 7:199].

[And Allah says]:

﴿ عَلَيْكُمْ لَا نَبْتَغِى ٱلْجَٰهِلِينَ ٥٥ ﴾

> "Peace be to you. We seek not the ignorant" [*al-Qaṣaṣ* 28:55].

Moreover, being occupied with teaching, writing, and spreading the *daʿwah* left me no time to respond to them. So let them say what they will. My sins are many. Perhaps their insults will lighten my burden and fall back upon them.

How true is the saying: "Allah has spared no one from harm, not even His Prophet of guidance, so what about me?"

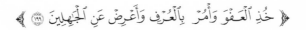

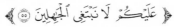

MY TEACHERS AND STUDIES

I STUDIED IN the [traditional primary school] until I completed the basic curriculum. Then Allah willed that some time passed without me seeking knowledge, as there was no one to encourage or support me. I used to love to seek knowledge and went to study at *al-Hādī* Mosque[6], but I was given no support. Then, after some time, I traveled to the land of al-Ḥaramayn (The Two Sacred Mosques) and Najd. I used to listen to the preachers, and their sermons amazed me. So I asked some of them which beneficial books to buy, and they recommended *Ṣaḥīḥ al-Bukhārī*, *Bulūgh al-Marām*, *Riyāḍ al-Ṣāliḥīn*, and *Fatḥ al-Majīd Sharḥ Kitāb al-Tawḥīd.* They also gave me copies of the materials from the Tawḥīd courses. At the time, I was working as a guard in a building in the al-Ḥujūn neighborhood of Makkah. I devoted myself to those books, and their contents stayed with me—especially *Fatḥ al-Majīd*—because much of what I read contradicted the practices common in my country.

After some time, I returned to my homeland. I rejected everything I saw that went against what I had learned from those books, such as sacrificing animals for other than Allah, building mausoleums over graves, and supplicating to the dead. This reached the Shi'ites, and they opposed what I was doing. One of them said, "Whoever changes his religion, kill him," while another sent a letter to my relatives saying, "If you do not stop him, we will imprison him." After that, they allowed me to enter al-Hādī Mosque to study with them, hoping to remove the *doubts* that had taken root in my heart. One of them repeated the poet's statement, "I felt love before I knew what it was./ It found my heart empty and stayed."

After that, I began studying with them in al-Hādī Mosque. The headteacher was the judge Muṭahhir Hanash. I studied *al-ʿAqd al-Thamīn*[7] and *al-Thalāthīn al-Mas'alah* and its explanation by Ḥābis[8]. One of our teachers there was Muḥammad b. Ḥasan al-Mutamayyiz. Once, we were studying the issue of *al-Ru'yah* (seeing Allah in the afterlife), and he began to ridicule Ibn al-Khuzaymah and others from the *Imāms* of *Ahl Al-Sunnah*. I kept my beliefs hidden. Unable to place my right hand over my left during prayer, I left them at my sides. We studied *Matn al-Azhār*[9] up to the book of *al-Nikāḥ* (marriage) and the explanation of *al-Farā'id*. It was a large tome above our level, so I did not benefit from it.

When I saw that the school's texts were not beneficial—save *al-Naḥw* (grammar)—I focused on studying *al-Ājurrūmiyyah*[10] and *Qaṭar al-Nadá*[11]. I then asked Judge Qāsim b. Yaḥyá Shuwayl to teach me *Bulūgh al-Marām*. We began, but the Shi'ites objected, so we stopped. Noticing that the course texts were Shi'ite and Muʿtazilite, I chose to focus on grammar instead. I studied Qaṭar al-Nadá several times with Ismāʿīl Ḥaṭbah—may Allah have mercy on him—at the mosque where I lived and where he prayed. He showed great care for us. At that time, Muḥammad b. Ḥūriyyah came to the *masjid*, and I advised him to leave off astrology. He urged [those over the *masjid*] to expel me. But some of them interceded on my behalf, and he remained quiet. Some of the Shi'ites would pass by while we were studying *Qaṭar al-Nadá* and say that my studies would not benefit me. But I stayed silent and continued gaining from grammar.

This continued until the revolution[12], and we left the country, settling in Najrān. I studied with Abū al-Ḥusayn Majd al-Dīn al-Mu'ayyid and benefited from him, specifically in Arabic. I remained in Najrān for about two years. When I was certain that the war between the Republic and the King's government was over worldly matters, I decided to travel to al-Ḥaramayn (Land of the Two Sacred Mosques) and Najd. I stayed in Najd for a month and a half in the institute of Qur'anic memorization, under *al-Shaykh* Muḥammad b. Sinān al-Ḥadā'ī—may Allah preserve him. He was very generous to me, seeing how much I was benefiting, and advised me to continue until he could send me to the Islamic University. But my situation changed in Riyāḍ, and I decided to travel to Makkah. I worked when I could find work and sought knowledge at night, attending *Shaykh* Yaḥyá b. ʿUthmān al-Pakistānī's lessons in *Tafsīr Ibn Kathīr*, *Ṣaḥīḥ al-Bukhārī*, and *Ṣaḥīḥ Muslim*. I studied various works and met two noble scholars from Yemen. The first was al-Qāḍī Yaḥyá al-Ashwal, with whom I studied *Subul al-Salām* by al-Ṣanʿānī. He would also teach me anything I asked. The second was *al-Shaykh* ʿAbd al-Razzāq al-Shāḥidhī al-Maḥwītī, who likewise taught me whatever I requested. After that, the Maʿhad al-Ḥaram al-Makkī (Institute of the

Ḥaram in Makkah) opened. I applied to take the entrance exam along with a group of students of knowledge and passed. All praise is due to Allah.

Among our most distinguished teachers was *al-Shaykh* ʿAbd al-ʿAzīz al-Subayyil [13]. I also studied with a group of students from the institute under *al-Shaykh* ʿAbd Allah b. Muḥammad b. Ḥumayd—may Allah have mercy on him—reading *al-Tuḥfah al-Saniyyah* after ʿIshá prayer in the Ḥaram. He would bring beneficial points from *Sharḥ Ibn ʿAqīl*[14] and other works. The material was above my classmates' level, so they stopped attending, and he—may Allah have mercy on him—discontinued the lesson. I also studied *al-Farāʾiḍ* (the laws of inheritance) with a group of students under *al-Shaykh* Muḥammad al-Subayyil—may Allah preserve him.

After settling in at the institute, I went to Najrān to bring my family, and we lived in Makkah during my six years of study. The lessons were held in the Ḥaram itself. And the blessing of studying in the *masājid* is well known. Do not even ask about the comfort and friendly atmosphere we experienced. The Messenger [of Allah] (ﷺ) spoke truthfully when he said, "No group gathers in one of Allah's houses to recite His Book and study it together except that tranquility descends upon them, angels surround them, mercy covers them, and Allah mentions them to those with Him."[15]

During the day, we studied at the institute, and each lesson served the correct creed and religion. From ʿAsr until after ʿIshá, we drank Zamzam water, about which the

Prophet (صَلَّى ٱللَّهُ عَلَيْهِ وَسَلَّمَ) said, "It is a drink that satisfies and a cure for illness."[16] We would listen to the preachers who had come from all over the country to perform *Ḥajj* or *ʿUmrah* (the lesser pilgrimage).

One of the teachers in the Ḥaram between Maghrib and ʿIshá was *al-Shaykh* ʿAbd al-ʿAzīz b. Rāshid al-Najdī, author of *Taysīr al-Waḥyayn fī al-Iqtiṣār ʿalá al-Ṣaḥīḥayn.* He made some errors in the book that we disagreed with. He used to say—may Allah have mercy on him—that the authentic narrations not found in the *Ṣaḥīḥayn* of al-Bukhārī and Muslim could be counted on one's fingers. I continued to disagree with this view until I decided to write *al-Ṣaḥīḥ al-Musnad mimmā laysa fī al-Ṣaḥīḥayn*, and through it, I became certain his statement was incorrect—may Allah have mercy on him.

He was—may Allah have mercy on him—a man of *Tawḥīd* with strong knowledge of ḥadīth, able to distinguish the authentic from the weak, the sound from the defective. His rejection of *al-Taqlīd* (blind following) amazed me—so much so that he wrote a treatise titled *al-Tawāghīt al-Muqannaʿah.* Some scholars asked him, "Did you mean us and the authorities in this treatise?" He replied, "If what's written in the book describes you, then it includes you. If not, then it doesn't." As a result, the book was later banned from entering the Kingdom. One night, he was asked to give a lesson, and perhaps it was a test. He began his lesson with the Statement of Allah:

﴿ ٱتَّبِعُواْ مَآ أُنزِلَ إِلَيۡكُم مِّن رَّبِّكُمۡ وَلَا تَتَّبِعُواْ مِن دُونِهِۦٓ أَوۡلِيَآءَۗ قَلِيلٗا مَّا تَذَكَّرُونَ ٣ ﴾

"Follow that which has been revealed to you from your Lord, and do not follow other than Him any *Awliya*. Little do you remember" [*al-A'rāf* 7:3].

He quoted several verses showing the prohibition of blind following, while some noble scholars were present. After that, he was barred from teaching in the Ḥaram. And Allah's help is sought.

One of the teachers I benefited from in the Ḥaram in Makkah was *al-Shaykh* Muḥammad b. ʿAbd Allah al-Sumālī. I attended his lessons for about seven months or more. He was—may Allah have mercy on him—a marvel (*ayah*) in his knowledge of the narrators of the two *Shaykhs*, al-Bukhārī and Muslim, and I benefited greatly from him in the science of ḥadīth. Praise be to my Lord. From the start of my studies, my only love has been for the knowledge of the Book and Sunnah.

After completing the intermediate and secondary levels at the Ḥaram Institute, focused entirely on religious studies, we moved to Madinah to attend the Islamic University. Most of us transferred to the College of *Da'wah wa Usūl al-Dīn* (Propagation and Fundamentals of the Religion). Among our most distinguished teachers were the two Egyptians: *al-Shaykh* al-Sayyid Muḥammad al-Ḥakīm and *al-Shaykh* Maḥmūd ʿAbd al-Wahhāb Fā'id.

When summer break came, I feared wasting time. So, I enrolled in the College of Sharīʿah for two reasons: first, to gain more knowledge; and second, because many of the lessons were similar—some even identical—to those in the College of Daʿwah, making it a useful review. Praise be to Allah, I completed both colleges and earned a dual degree. However, Allah be praised, I do not concern myself with degrees. In my view, it is knowledge that truly deserves recognition.

The year I completed both colleges, the university launched its advanced studies program, what they call a master's degree. I applied for the interview and, praise be to Allah, I passed. The degree was a specialization in ḥadīth, and praise be to Allah, I benefited from what I love. Among our most prominent teachers were *al-Shaykh* Muḥammad al-Amīn al-Miṣrī—may Allah have mercy on him—*al-Shaykh* Muḥammad al-Ḥakīm al-Miṣrī, and toward the end of the program, *al-Shaykh* Ḥammād al-Anṣārī. Some nights, I would attend *al-Shaykh* ʿAbd al-Azīz b. Bāz's *Ṣaḥīḥ Muslim* lesson in the Ḥaram. I also attended some of *al-Shaykh* al-Albānī's private sessions with other students to benefit.

When I was in the Ḥaram in Makkah, I would teach some students *Qaṭar al-Nadá* and *al-Tuḥfah al-Saniyyah*. In Madinah, I taught some of my brothers *al-Tuḥfah al-Saniyyah* in the Ḥaram and promised others to teach *Jāmiʿ al-Tirmidhī*, *Qaṭar al-Nadá*, and *al-Bāʾith al-Ḥathīth* at my home after ʿAsr.

The *da'wah* spread far and wide from Madinah, reaching the *dunya* in just six years. Some generous individuals financed it, while Muqbil b. Hādī and a few of his brothers devoted themselves to teaching their fellow Muslims. The *da'wah* trips across the Kingdom were a joint effort by the brothers—students of knowledge, to grow and teach others, and the common folk, to learn. As a result, many people benefited and grew to love the *da'wah*.

One of our brothers from among the students was the *imām* of a *masjid* in Riyāḍ. Some scholars criticized him for using a *sutrah*. He replied, "We cannot convince you. By Allah, even a common person could stand and teach you the *aḥādīth* on the *sutrah*." So, he called one of the lay brothers who loved the *da'wah* and had memorized the narrations on the *sutrah* from *al-Lu'lu' wa al-Marjān fīmā Ittafaqa 'alayhi al-Shaykhān*[17]. He stood and related those narrations. Those who had opposed him felt ashamed and remained silent. After this, the blind followers and corrupt scholars stirred. These blind followers—seen as scholars by the people—were unsettled when even our younger students asked, "Who collected this ḥadīth?" and "What is its condition?" Questions they were not used to, which embarrassed them before the common folk. Sometimes, the student would tell them, "This narration is not authentic. So-and-so and so-and-so are in the chain of transmission, and so-and-so has graded it weak." They were overwhelmed, as if the world had closed in on them. They began falsely claiming that these students were Kharijites, though the brothers were nothing of the sort. They did not declare Muslims disbelievers over sins or permit their blood, as the *Khawārij* do. Still, some newer brothers made mistakes, as beginners are often overly zealous.

At that time, I was studying for my master's thesis, and one night, before I knew it, I was arrested along with about one-hundred and fifty other people. Some escaped. The earth shook between those who stood with us and those who did not. We remained in the prison for close to a month and half. After this, we were set free. Thereafter, some treatises from Juhaymān[18] appeared, and a group of us were arrested. During the interrogation, they told me, "You wrote [these treatises]. Juhaymān is unable to write." I disavowed the allegation, and Allah knows I neither wrote those statements nor helped write them. After three months in prison, an order was issued to deport the foreigners.

When I arrived in Yemen, I returned to my village, teaching the children the *Qur'ān*. I felt as if the *dunya* were closing in on me, as though I were accused of trying to destroy the Religion, the country, and its rulers. I knew no one in authority or from the tribes. I would simply say, "Allah is sufficient for me and the best of protectors." When things became difficult, I would travel to Sanʿā, Ḥāshid, or Dhimār, and also to Taʿiz, Ibb, and al-Ḥudaydah for *daʿwah* or to visit my brothers for the sake of Allah.

Later, a generous person sent my library from Madinah. When it reached Markaz Kadam, they demanded five hundred Saudi riyals from him. He refused, thinking it was a bribe. But he didn't realize that the wrongdoing was on their part, not his, for a bribe is given to uphold falsehood or to deny a rightful claim.

Some of our companions went to get the books, and [the official] told them, "Allah willing, come back after the *Ẓuhr* prayer. But after *Ẓuhr*, they discovered that the Shi'ites had mobilized and asked the authorities not to release them because they were "*Wahhābī*" books.[19] Do not ask about the fines, hardships, and injustices I suffered. Many of the brothers from my land made great efforts to follow up on the matter, including *al-Shaykh* ʿAbd Allah b. Ḥusayn al-Aḥmar, *al-Shaykh* Hazāʾ Ḍabʿān, and those overseeing the Office of Counseling and Guidance, among them, Judge Yaḥyá al-Fasayyal—may Allah have mercy on him—and our brother ʿĀ'id b. ʿAlī Mismār. After much difficulty, the people of Saʾdah sent a telegram to President ʿAlī b. ʿAbd Allah b. Ṣāliḥ, who referred the matter to Judge ʿAlī al-Samān. He sent me a letter promising to release the books and said, "The people of Saʾdah are harsh. They declare the scholars of Sanʿā disbelievers." When the books arrived in Sanʿā, it happened that Judge ʿAlī al-Samān was abroad. So, the brothers went to the head of the Ministry of Endowments, who told them, "The books need to be inspected." Some of our brothers went to the Office of Counseling and Guidance to retrieve the books. The office responded, "This falls under our responsibility. We will inspect them. Whatever aligns with the Religion, we will hand over to al-Wādiʿī. Whatever contradicts it, we will confiscate." And since they knew the books were purely religious, they gave them to us without inspection. May Allah reward them with good. I brought the books home. Praise be to Allah. My relatives then built a small library and masjid—may Allah reward them with good. They said, "We will pray here to avoid trouble." At times, only about six of us would gather to pray.

At that time, the governor, Hādī al-Hashishī, summoned me. So, I went to *al-Shaykh* Qā'id Majlī—may Allah have mercy on him—and he called the governor, asking, "What do you want with al-Wādi'ī?"

"Only to make his acquaintance," the governor said.

"We will go up to see him at his institute," *al-Shaykh* Qā'id said.

On another occasion, someone from the authorities summoned me. Ḥusayn b. Qā'id Majlī went in with me and spoke about the Shi'ites, explaining that we call to the Book of Allah and the Sunnah, and that the Shi'ites oppose us out of fear that their true beliefs will be exposed. The official replied, "Indeed, the Shi'ites have darkened Yemen's history. As long as your *da'wah* is as you say, then continue, and we are with you." After this, I remained in my library. After only a few short days, some Egyptian brothers arrived and began lessons from the books of *Ḥadith* and Arabic language. Students continued to come from Egypt, Kuwait, al-Ḥaramayn and Najd, Aden, Ḥadarah-Mawt, Algeria, Libya, Somalia, Belgium, and many Islamic and non-Islamic lands.

Presently, the number of students is between six hundred and seven hundred, among which are around one hundred and seventy families. Allah provides for them from His Bounty. None of this comes from our own strength, knowledge, courage, or eloquence. Rather, Allah has decreed it, and all praise is due to Him for granting it to us.

THE LESSONS

OUR classes:

1. *Tafsīr Ibn Kathīr* after *al-Ẓuhr*
2. *Ṣaḥīḥ al-Bukhārī* after *al-'Asr*
3. *Ṣaḥīḥ Muslim* followed by *Mustadrak al-Ḥākim* between *Maghrib* and *'Ishá*
4. *Al- Ṣaḥīḥ al-Musnad mimmá laysa fī al- Ṣaḥīḥayn* before *al-Ẓuhr*
5. *Al- Ṣaḥīḥ al-Musnad min Dalā'il al-Nubuwwah*
6. *Al-Jāmi' al- Ṣaḥīḥ fī al-Qadr*
7. Previously, I was teaching *Sharḥ Ibn 'Aqīl*, but fell ill and had to leave it.

As for our brothers in Islām, they hold lessons for others in all areas of study, according to the students' level—in *Tawḥīd*, *'Aqīdah* (creed), *Fiqh* and its principles, Ḥadīth and its methodology, *al-Farā'iḍ* (inheritance law), grammar, handwriting, dictation, and everything a student needs from the religious sciences. When the *masjid* and living quarters become overcrowded, the lessons take place in the valley under the trees: beneficial knowledge and a pleasant atmosphere, and the Favor is from Allah alone.

WRITINGS

Abū ʿAbd al-Raḥmān leaned more toward research and writing than toward other fields. At first, he was fond of extensively tracing sources, but later came to see that compiling weak narrations merely for citation was not the way of the *Salaf*. In fact, they would not even gather all the authentic chains. That is why *Ṣaḥīḥ al-Bukhārī*, *Ṣaḥīḥ Muslim*, *Sunan Abī Dāwūd*, *Jāmiʿ al-Tirmidhī*, *Sunan al-Nasāʾī*, *Sunan Ibn Mājah*, and other collections of Islām were compiled this way, and their authors were the great memorizers and the exemplars in this discipline.

As for me—praise be to Allah—I do not judge a ḥadīth to be weak without thorough study. I examine its chains of transmission and sources and compare the views of the early scholars. I often return to the books of *ʿilal* (hidden defects) and try to present practical, accessible knowledge for the reader. As for those who are only prepared to criticize, let them bring forth weak hadiths that I have authenticated or authentic hadiths that I have declared weak.

Praise be to Allah, I remain engaged in writing alongside teaching and calling to Allah. I praise Allah, for I am occupied with writing, calling to Allah, and teaching, unlike many others. Some devote themselves to *daʿwah* without giving any attention to knowledge and teaching. Others focus on teaching but pay no attention to *daʿwah* and writing. And others busy themselves with writing and verification while neglecting both *daʿwah* and teaching altogether. As for our brothers [in Dammaj], they are callers, writers, verifiers, guards, and cooks. They take on the duty of teaching their brothers. All praise and favor belong to Allah alone. He is the one who aided them in all of this.

RELIGIOUS VERDICTS

Requests for religious verdicts have come to me from across the Islamic world and beyond. About a year ago, I became too busy to respond to them all and had to reduce the number I answered. May Allah forgive me for my shortcomings.

INQUIRIES ABOUT THE INSTITUTE

Letters arrive from many Islamic countries and beyond, asking about the institute, what is taught there, and what the admission requirements are. We respond to them by saying that the government requires a daily financial penalty for anyone who does not carry a residency permit and does not grant residency to students of the institute unless their government allows it.

LOVE OF THE RIGHTEOUS FOR THE DAʿWAH

By Allah's grace, everyone among the righteous who hears about the *daʿwah* and those who visit love and support it. The letters I've received attest to this. They all make *du'a* for the *daʿwah* and for those who uphold it…We praise Allah, Glorified and Exalted is He. Most Muslims—those who love truth and reject fanaticism—find joy in the call of *Ahl al-Sunnah*. They trust it and none other.

THE ENMITY OF THE OPPONENTS OF ISLAM AND THE INNOVATORS TOWARD THE DAʿWAH

The greatest opponents of the *daʿwah* are as follows:

The communists, who attack the *daʿwah* and publish slanderous articles in newspapers such as *al-ʿUmmāl* and *al-Thawrī*, both of which are published in the south.

Also, the Mukaramah of Najrān, who are in greater disbelief than the Jews and Christians, are among the most hostile to the *daʿwah*. They try to harm it in every way, but Allah repels them.

Likewise, the *Shīʿah* and the *Ṣūfīs*, all of whom work to turn people away from the *daʿwah*. But Allah refuses except to complete His light, even if the liars hate it.

Similarly, the partisans (*ḥizbīs*), such as the bankrupt Muslim Brotherhood and their offshoots: *Jamʿiyyah al-Iṣlāḥ*, *Jamʿiyyah al-Ḥikmah*, and the *Surūrī Jamʿiyyah al-Iḥsān*.

And with this, we conclude what we intended to write. All praise is due to Allah, the Lord of the worlds.

One of Shaykh Muqbil's old rooms

The Shaykh's masjid in Dammāj

APPENDIX I

THE SCHOLARS' PRAISE OF SHAYKH MUQBIL

THE NOBLE SCHOLAR OF ISLĀM, *al-ʿAllāmah* Rabīʿ b. Hādī al-Madkhalī said, "He is the *ʿAllāmah, al-Muḥaddith, al-Mujāhid*, reviver of the *Salafī* call in Yemen, *al-Shaykh* Muqbil b. Hādī b. Qā'idah al-Hamdānī, al-Wādiʿī from the tribe of Āli Rāshid.

He was an unsheathed sword against the people of falsehood, from the *Rāfidis*, communists, *Sūfis*, and deviant sects. He established the *Salafī* call in the best manner and founded a scholarly *Salafī* school named Dār al-Ḥadīth. It attracted students from across Yemen—and even beyond, from Arab and Islamic countries, as well as Europe and America. He was a shining example for [his students]—that upright, modest, ascetic mountain, Muqbil b. Hādī al-Wādiʿī, whose life reminds us of the biographies of the *Salaf*, especially *Imām* Aḥmad."[20]

At the end of *Shaykh* Muqbil's biography, *Shaykh* Rabīʿ states, "I knew this man for his truthfulness, sincerity, humility, detachment from worldly things, sound creed, and firm *Salafī* methodology. He would return to the truth, whether it came from the young or the old. Allah blessed his *daʿwah*, and the people embraced it. He and his students had a profound impact on the people of Yemen, a fact recognized by all who possess intellect, faith, and fairness."[21]

Shortly after *Shaykh* Muqbil's death, *al-ʿAllāmah* Rabīʾ b. Hādī stated in some advice to the people of Yemen, We offer our condolences on the passing of the flag bearer of Sunnah and Tawḥīd, the true caller to Allah, the reviver of the faith in the land of Yemen.

The effects of his call reached far and wide across the earth. In truth, I say to you that your land, after the era of the best generations, came to know the *Sunnah* and the *Salafī* methodology at various times and to varying degrees. Yet I do not know of any period that compares to this one, when Allah blessed you and the people of Yemen through this righteous man: the *muḥaddith*, the ascetic, the devout, who trampled the worldly life and its adornments beneath his feet."[22]

THE *MUḤADDITH, IMĀM* Muḥammad Nāṣir al-Dīn al-Albānī stated, "As for *al-Shaykh* Muqbil, the people of Makkah are more knowledgeable of its mountains. The reports you have brought us about him are the strongest proof that Allah granted him success. And perhaps, among the callers of our time across the earth, he has no equal."[23]

THE *IMĀM, AL-FAQĪH*, ʿAbd al-Azīz Ibn Bāz was asked by a person from Yemen, "Where should I go to study?" The *Shaykh* replied, "Go to *Shaykh* Muqbil."[24]

Shaykh Muqbil related, "At that time, a man had fled to Riyāḍ and went to *Shaykh* Ibn Bāz, saying, "O *Shaykh*, I am from the people of the *Sunnah*, but I have no documents." The *Shaykh* replied, "Prove to me you are from the people of the *Sunnah*." The man pulled out a piece of paper with a reference from me. Upon seeing it, the *Shaykh* wrote him a letter that allowed him to travel."[25]

THE *IMĀM*, *al-'Allāmah* Muḥammad b. Ṣāliḥ al-'Uthaymīn stated, "Indeed, I hold *Shaykh* Muqbil to be an *Imām*."[26]

THE *IMĀM*, *al-'Allāmah* Aḥmad b. Yaḥyá al-Najmī stated, "Praise be to Allah for His Divine Decree. This calls for patience, as death comes to every soul. But whoever leaves behind a legacy like his is not truly gone. He established the call, brought about reform, spread the truth, and strove with admirable effort. We consider him among the righteous, and Allah will judge us all. Yet what we see with our eyes and witness with our senses is clear: he did much good, and few have achieved what he did. These centers spread throughout Yemen are nothing but a part of his legacy. Indeed, they are from the fruits of his good deeds…"[27]

THE NOBLE *SHAYKH*, *al-'Allāmah* Ṣāliḥ al-Fawzān said, "Yes, *Shaykh* Muqbil—may Allah have mercy on him—studied here in this country at the Islamic University. He learned Tawḥīd and then returned to Yemen, where he called to Allah and to Tawḥīd. From what I have heard, and from the clear fruits of his *da'wah*, it was a call grounded in goodness. May Allah have mercy on him."[28]

APPENDIX II

SELECTED BIBLIOGRAPHY OF THE SHAYKH'S WORKS

Tafsīr:

1. A verification and study of the chains of narration in *Tafsīr Ibn Kathīr* up to Sūrah al-Mā'idah, compiled in two volumes. The remainder of the work was completed by a group of the *Shaykh's* students.
2. *Al-Ṣaḥīḥ al-Musnad min Asbāb al-Nuzūl* (*Authentic Musnad of the Reasons for Revelation*): The *Shaykh* explained that what motivated him to write this work was "the joining of two great disciplines: the *tafsīr* of the Book of Allah and the Sunnah of the Messenger of Allah." He also noted that "knowing the reason for a verse's revelation helps in understanding its meaning."[29]

Al-Aqīdah (Creed):

3. *Al-Shafā'ah* (The Book of Intercession): In the introduction to the third edition, the *Shaykh* writes, "This book serves as a refutation of the innovators. The introduction brings together relevant Qur'ānic verses and clarifies the difference between accepted and rejected forms of intercession. The book also refutes those who seek intercession from those who do not

possess it, such as the *Sufis*, extreme *Shiʿites*, *Rāfiḍīs*, and others."[30]

4. *Al-Jāmiʿ al-Ṣaḥīḥ fī al-Qadr* (*Authentic Jāmiʿ Regarding the Divine Decree*): This book comprises hundreds of pieces of evidence establishing the correct belief in Allah's Decree. In the introduction to the book, the *Shaykh* states, "Indeed, Allah has decreed both good and evil. So, I sought Allah's help in compiling a selection of Qur'ānic verses and Prophetic traditions, and I titled it *Al-Jāmiʿ al-Ṣaḥīḥ fī al-Qadr*. I ask Allah to make it a benefit to Islām and the Muslims."[31]
5. *Al-Ṣaḥīḥ al-Musnad min Dalā'il al-Nubuwwah* (*Authentic Musnad of the Proofs of Prophethood*): Concerning this book, the *Shaykh* stated, "Indeed, studying the proofs of Prophethood strengthens the believer's faith and, by Allah's will, may lead someone to embrace Islām."[32]
6. *Rudūd Ahl al-ʿIlm alá al-Ṭāʿinīna fī Ḥadīth al-Siḥr* (*The Scholars' Refutation of Those Who Reproach the Ḥadīth of Magic*): This book repudiates those who reject the authentic tradition of our mother A'ishah, in which she relates the story of a spell being cast on the Messenger of Allah (ﷺ). The *Shaykh* states, "When I was in the city of the Messenger of Allah, news reached me that some people were rejecting the authenticity of the ḥadīth about the Prophet being affected by magic. I said to the one who informed me that the narration is found in Bukhārī and Muslim. He

replied, "They still reject it." This, the *Shaykh* says, is what moved him to write this clarification: "I do not claim to have authenticated this narration. It was already authentic long before I came into existence."[33]

7. *Al-Makhraj min al-Fitnah* (*The Escape from Tribulation*): This work refutes several deviant sects and their false ideologies. The *Shaykh* also stresses the importance of the Muslim *Ummah* unifying upon the Book and Sunnah and warns from the plot of *al-Shayṭān* to plant the seeds of separation and fanatical partisanship.[34] In earlier editions of this treatise, the *Shaykh* made some remarks about the Kingdom of Saudi Arabia. However, as *al-Shaykh*, *al-ʿAllāmah* Rabīʾ b. Hādī points out in his biography of our *Shaykh*, "He retracted his [earlier] opinion of the Saudi government in an article entitled '*Bara'ah al-Dhimmah*.'" [See Appendix III.]
8. *Hādhihi Daʿwatuna wa Aqīdatuna* (*This is our Call and Our Creed*): This concise treatise is a clarification of the *Shaykh's daʿwah* in Yemen, covering matters of *al-Tawḥīd*, Divine Decree, love of the Prophet's Companions, hatred for rhetoric and its people, and so on. He states in the treatise, "Our call and creed is more beloved to us than our own selves, possessions, and children. We are not prepared to sell it for gold or silver. We state this so that no one will have any hopes of buying us with the *dirham* and *dinar*." [See Appendix V.]
9. *Īdāḥ al-Maqāl fī Asbāb al-Zilzāl* (*Clarification of the Causes of Earthquakes*): This treatise establishes the

reasons for earthquakes, as found in the Book of Allah and the authentic Sunnah. It also refutes those from the heretics and disbelievers who attribute these occurrences to "natural disasters."

Hadith and its Sciences:

10. *Al-Ṣaḥīḥ al-Musnad mimmá laysa fī al- Al-Ṣaḥīḥayn*: In the introduction, *Shaykh* Muqbil states, "To me, reading the *Ṣaḥīḥayn* (of al-Bukhārī and Muslim) is the sweetest pleasure in the world. When I open Bukhārī and read, 'ʿAbd Allāh ibn Yūsuf narrated to us: Mālik narrated to us...' or see Imām Muslim write, 'Yaḥyā ibn Yaḥyā narrated to us...,' I forget all the worries and problems of the *dunya* (world)."
11. *Al-Jāmiʾ al-Ṣaḥīḥ mimmá laysa fī al-Ṣaḥīḥayn* (*Authentic Jāmiʾ of Traditions That Are Not in the Ṣaḥīḥayn*): The *Shaykh* arranged and chaptered this collection according the *Ṣaḥīḥ* of *al-Imām* al-Bukhārī.
12. *Sharʿiyyah al-Ṣalah fī al-Niʿāl* (*The Legality of Performing Prayer in Shoes*)
13. *Tuḥfah al-Shabāb al-Rabbānī*: This treatise is a refutation of *al-Imam* al-Shawkānī concerning the issue of masturbation.
14. *Taḥrīm Taṣwīr Dhawāt al-Arwāḥ*, (*The Prohibition of Depicting Animate Beings*): In this work, the *Shaykh* states, "Among the tribulations the Muslims have been tested with are pictures. There is hardly a home without them. They have even reached the Bedouins in the

valleys and on the mountaintops. The cause of this is the Muslims' neglect of their religion."

15. *Dhamm al-Mas'alah* (*The Dispraiseworthy Nature of Begging*)

APPENDIX III

WHAT I WITNESSED IN THE KINGDOM OF SAUDI ARABIA

ALL PRAISE IS DUE TO Allah, Lord of the worlds; and may the peace and blessings be upon our Prophet Muḥammad (صَلَّى ٱللَّٰهُ عَلَيْهِ وَسَلَّمَ), his family, and all his companions. I testify that nothing has the right to be worshipped besides Allah, and I testify that Muḥammad is His servant and Messenger.

To proceed: I have been reluctant for some time to speak about the subject I am about to address. However, my resolve grew stronger, as I feared I might die before freeing myself from this.

It had been suggested to me more than once to seek permission from *Amīr* Aḥmad, the vice minister of Internal Affairs [in the Kingdom Saudi Arabia], to make *Ḥajj* and *ʿUmrah*. But I replied to the brothers that I have no need of that, and told myself that I would not allow myself to be belittled, since I was at ease in my country among my students, and praise is for Allah.

Then Allah decreed that I fell ill and received treatment at al-Thawrah Hospital in Sanʿā. Afterward, the doctors decided I needed to travel abroad. One of them said, "We advise you to travel to Saudi, because they are advanced in medical care."

I was going to Saudi Arabia, despite having spoken against them in more than one recording. I agreed to go because, despite our differences, it is better than going to the adversaries of Islām. So after that, permission was sought on my behalf, and the noble *Shaykh*, *al-ʿAllāmah* Muḥammad ibn Ṣāliḥ al-ʿUthaymīn interceded for me. His intercession was accepted, allowing me to enter the country for treatment. Praise be to Allah, the Saudi Embassy arranged all of my affairs.

By and by, we arrived in Riyāḍ and were received by officials from the Ministry of Internal Affairs, who had paid for a hotel for us. May Allah reward them with good. This was more than we had expected, and they were extremely generous to us. They quickly admitted me to the hospital, where I witnessed their great generosity toward us. Our brothers would sit with us—praise be to Allah—and we would engage in discussions focused solely on knowledge, avoiding all other topics.

And praise be to Allah, I am not among those who repay good with harm or generosity with offense. Allah be praised, brothers would come and ask me about *aḥādīth*, and I would ask them questions in return. At that time, I was admitted to the hospital and remained there for about ten days. They then said, "O Abū ʿAbd al-Raḥmān, you must travel abroad." So I said, "*Khayran*, Allah willing." We arrived in Jeddah and were received in a hotel called '*Funduq al-Hamrah*.' May Allah reward *Amīr* Nāyif, the Minister of Internal Affairs, with good, since we were received and treated so hospitably. May Allah grant him good.

After that, I requested a meeting with him, and praise be to Allah, it was a pleasant and insightful encounter, one with a man of intelligence. If you were to review matters of knowledge with him, you would find he possesses a good share of understanding. Praise be to Allah. He then said to me, "Whichever country you wish to go to, Allah willing, we will arrange everything for you." But since I had no experience in such matters, I replied, "You choose." So, he chose America, as it is more advanced than other countries in treating liver diseases.

Later, I was amazed when I went to Makkah. In Yemen, I had about four guards at my door, yet I still did not feel safe in my own home, neither by day nor by night. But in Makkah, I stayed at a hotel called Dār al-Azhar, and on nights when I couldn't sleep, I would go alone to the Ḥaram in the middle of the night. Nothing compares to the blessing of the peace and comfort I felt. I would go out by myself, make *ṭawāf*, pray, stay as long as I liked, and then return to my room.

I have not experienced this level of security in any other country. The reason for this is the steadfast adherence to the Book of Allah and the Sunnah of the Messenger of Allah (صَلَّى ٱللَّهُ عَلَيْهِ وَسَلَّمَ) by the authorities and many of the citizens. And our Lord spoke the truth when He said in His Noble Book about the people of the Scripture:

﴿وَلَوْ أَنَّهُمْ أَقَامُوا۟ ٱلتَّوْرَىٰةَ وَٱلْإِنجِيلَ وَمَآ أُنزِلَ إِلَيْهِم مِّن
رَّبِّهِمْ لَأَكَلُوا۟ مِن فَوْقِهِمْ وَمِن تَحْتِ أَرْجُلِهِم ۚ مِّنْهُمْ أُمَّةٌ
مُّقْتَصِدَةٌ ۖ وَكَثِيرٌ مِّنْهُمْ سَآءَ مَا يَعْمَلُونَ ﴿٦٦﴾﴾

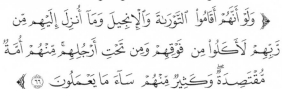

> "And if they had only established the *Tawrāh* and the *Injīl* and that which has (now) been sent down to them from their Lord, they would surely have gotten provision from above them and from beneath their feet" [*al-Mā'idah* 5:66].

And He says:

﴿ وَلَوْ أَنَّ أَهْلَ ٱلْقُرَىٰٓ ءَامَنُوا۟ وَٱتَّقَوْا۟ لَفَتَحْنَا عَلَيْهِم بَرَكَٰتٍ مِّنَ ٱلسَّمَآءِ وَٱلْأَرْضِ ﴿٩٦﴾ ﴾

> "If the people of the towns had only believed and had *taqwa*, we would have indeed opened up for them blessings from the heavens and the earth" [*al-ʿArāf* 7:96].

And He says about *Quraysh*:

﴿ وَقَالُوٓا۟ إِن نَّتَّبِعِ ٱلْهُدَىٰ مَعَكَ نُتَخَطَّفْ مِنْ أَرْضِنَآ ﴿٥٧﴾ ﴾

> "And they said: 'If we were to follow the guidance with you, we would be snatched away from our land" [*al-Qaṣaṣ* 28:57].

And He says:

﴿ أَوَلَمْ نُمَكِّن لَّهُمْ حَرَمًا ءَامِنًا يُجْبَىٰٓ إِلَيْهِ ثَمَرَٰتُ كُلِّ شَىْءٍ رِّزْقًا مِّن لَّدُنَّا ﴿٥٧﴾ ﴾

"Have We not established for them a secure sanctuary, to which are brought fruits of all kinds, a provision from Us?" [*al- Qaṣaṣ* 28:57]

And He says:

﴿ أَوَلَمْ يَرَوْاْ أَنَّا جَعَلْنَا حَرَمًا ءَامِنًا وَيُتَخَطَّفُ ٱلنَّاسُ مِنْ حَوْلِهِمْ ٦٧ ﴾

"Have they not seen that We have made [Makkah] a secure sanctuary, while the people all around them are being snatched away?" [*al-ʿAnkabūt* 29:67]

And He also said in His Noble Book:

﴿ وَأَلَّوِ ٱسْتَقَٰمُواْ عَلَى ٱلطَّرِيقَةِ لَأَسْقَيْنَٰهُم مَّآءً غَدَقًا ١٦ ﴾

"And if they had only remained upright upon the Path, We would have given them water (rain) in abundance" [*al-Jinn* 72:16].

And our Lord spoke the truth when He said in His Noble Book:

﴿ وَعَدَ ٱللَّهُ ٱلَّذِينَ ءَامَنُواْ مِنكُمْ وَعَمِلُواْ ٱلصَّٰلِحَٰتِ لَيَسْتَخْلِفَنَّهُمْ فِى ٱلْأَرْضِ كَمَا ٱسْتَخْلَفَ ٱلَّذِينَ مِن قَبْلِهِمْ وَلَيُمَكِّنَنَّ لَهُمْ دِينَهُمُ ٱلَّذِى ٱرْتَضَىٰ لَهُمْ وَلَيُبَدِّلَنَّهُم مِّنۢ بَعْدِ خَوْفِهِمْ أَمْنًا يَعْبُدُونَنِى لَا يُشْرِكُونَ بِى شَيْئًا ٥٥ ﴾

> "Allah has promised those amongst you who believe and work righteous deeds that He will indeed grant them authority in the earth, the way He gave authority to those before them. And He will establish for them their religion that He has chosen for them. And He will exchange their fear with security, so that they can worship Me and not ascribe any partners with Me" [*al-Nūr* 24:55].

And He says in His Noble Book:

﴿ لِإِيلَٰفِ قُرَيْشٍ ١ إِۦلَٰفِهِمْ رِحْلَةَ ٱلشِّتَآءِ وَٱلصَّيْفِ ٢ فَلْيَعْبُدُوا۟ رَبَّ هَٰذَا ٱلْبَيْتِ ٣ ٱلَّذِىٓ أَطْعَمَهُم مِّن جُوعٍ وَءَامَنَهُم مِّنْ خَوْفٍۭ ٤ ﴾

> "It is a great Grace and protection from Allah for the protection of the *Quraysh*. We cause the *Quraysh* caravans to set forth safe in winter and in summer. So, let them worship Allah, the Lord of this House, Who has fed them against hunger and has made them safe from fear" [*Quraysh* 106:1-4].

Thus, safety and security are great blessings from Allah, and their cause is steadfastness upon the Book of Allah and the Sunnah of His Messenger (ﷺ). Because this country has remained steadfast, Allah has granted it stability, and all praise is due to Allah.

We ask Allah to bless them with righteous advisors, protect them from evil companions who beautify falsehood, and guide them to keep the company of people of goodness and virtue, even if they hear words that may be difficult to accept. As it is said, "Your true friend is the one who speaks the truth to you, not the one who always agrees with you, for that person is your enemy.'

So, we must praise Allah, and it is likewise obligatory upon the people of this country to do so—for there are some among them, perhaps, who are corrupt and seek to spread immorality. May Allah reward the authorities with goodness. I saw in the newspaper that *Amīr* Nāyif was asked about allowing women to run for office. He replied, "Do you want the men to stay at home while the women go out and take charge? No, don't even try it." He was also asked about implementing elections and said, "We haven't seen them succeed in neighboring countries. It's always the wealthy and influential who come out on top." And he spoke the truth. Moreover, [elections] came to us from the adversaries of Islām. Many welcomed the Human Rights Society, despite the falsehood it promotes, calling the *ḥudūd* (prescribed punishments) barbaric, rejecting the Book and the Sunnah, and replacing them with systems from the opponents of Islām.

The Saudi government—may Allah grant them success in all good—only received the Human Rights Society on the condition that it comply with Islām, the Book of Allah, and the Sunnah, and uphold the implementation of the *ḥudūd*, as our Lord says in His Noble Book:

﴿ وَلَكُمۡ فِي ٱلۡقِصَاصِ حَيَوٰةٞ ﴾

> "And in the establishment of the *Qiṣāṣ* (the Law of Equality in punishment) there is life for you" [*al-Baqarah* 2:179].

Murder is rare in this country, and so is theft. You can leave your car by the masjid or at your front door, and no one will come to steal it. But in other countries, if you leave it, you might not find it when you return. In fact, they might even steal a person's car while he's still inside it. This is the reason for establishing the *ḥudūd*. May Allah reward them with good.

As you heard earlier in the verse: "And in the establishment of Qiṣāṣ, there is life for you." So, if a thief knows that his hand will be cut off for stealing, it will deter him from doing so. And if a fornicator knows he will be lashed if unmarried, or stoned if married or previously married, then fornication will decrease. I'm not saying it would disappear completely, but it would become rare.

In addition, forming the Committee for the Promotion of Virtue and the Prevention of Vice is noteworthy. I read in the newspaper that King Fahd provided the Committee with around three hundred vehicles and said to them, "You are the committee of restraint, and you are accountable before Allah." By doing so, they have done well—for their country and themselves.

Indeed, it is an obligation upon every Muslim in all Islamic lands to support this government, even if only by speaking a good word about it. Its enemies are many, both from within and without. There are also people of desire and corruption within it, but Allah has subdued them through the establishment of this blessed state, and all praise is due to Allah. Therefore, it is obligatory upon every Muslim to assist this government.

Qiṣāṣ, along with the other *ḥudūd*, is a blessing from Allah upon society. Some criticize us for establishing one of Allah's prescribed punishments while they themselves annihilate entire nations. These *ḥudūd* are, in reality, a benefit for both the individual and society. For the individual, they serve as an expiation, as mentioned in the *Ṣaḥīḥayn* on the authority of ʿUbādah ibn Ṣāmit. As for society, the *ḥudūd* serve as a protection for their property, blood, and honor. You can go to the seashore or any public place and see that a man and his wife do not fear their safety. These *ḥudūd* are truly beneficial. But when they were abandoned in many Islamic countries, people became unable to control theft, crime, intoxicants, and drugs. The cause of this is the neglect of the *ḥudūd*. Allah *al-musta'ān*.

Another virtue is their effort to build masājid in Islamic and non-Islamic countries. However, I advise them: when they build a masjid, they should entrust it to *Ahl al-Sunnah*. If they give it to a *Sufi*, he may insult them and use his sermons to attack them. If they give it to a *ḥizbī* (partisan), he will turn it into a platform for *ḥizbiyyah*. So, we advise them to give the *masājid* to *Ahl al-Sunnah*, those who love this government and support its leadership.

Next is the issue of what I previously wrote and said in recordings—something I've been asked about more than once. I have instructed the brother responsible for printing my books not to include any of my past statements against Saudi Arabia. Allah says in His Noble Book:

﴿ هَلْ جَزَآءُ ٱلْإِحْسَٰنِ إِلَّا ٱلْإِحْسَٰنُ ٦٠ ﴾

"Should the reward for good be anything else but good?" [*al-Raḥmān* 55:60]

They have shown me kindness and generosity, and we are not among those who repay good with harm. This is one of the blessings of Allah.

Let me also say, no one has pushed me nor forced me to say this. Rather, I myself consider it an obligation to free myself from it.

Yes, I spoke out and believe I was wrongly expelled from the Kingdom. Yet, Lā ilāha illa Allah, how often I argued with those who declared the Saudi rulers disbelievers, saying to them, "The Saudi government is not a disbelieving government." I used to teach lessons that never touched on such issues—praise be to Allah. But one must practice patience and forgiveness. And since they—may Allah reward them with good—have pardoned me, I too must pardon.

They also give great importance to the care of Ḥajj pilgrims and the expansion of the Two Sacred Mosques, following the example of the Messenger of Allah

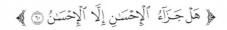

(صَلَّى ٱللَّهُ عَلَيْهِ وَسَلَّمَ) said, "Whoever builds a masjid for the Sake of Allah, Allah will build for him the like in *Jannah*."[35] They also show great care for the Ḥajj pilgrims, ensuring their safety by placing security at the entrances of the Ḥaram. When the fires broke out recently, they responded by providing non-flammable tents. May Allah reward them with good for their concern and dedication. When we were in Mina, aircrafts would circle overhead to monitor and protect the pilgrims. May Allah reward them well for this care.

I say, if you were to read the books of the early scholars and the history of Makkah, you would find that Abū Ṭāhir al-Qarmaṭī killed around thirty thousand people in total, in the Ḥaram and its surrounding areas. In some years, the pilgrims from Egypt were barred; in others, those from Iraq or Yemen were turned away. But after the establishment of the Saudi government—praise be to Allah—we find that they have protected both friend and foe who come for Ḥajj, treating them as guests of al-Raḥmān, and as their own guests as well. May Allah reward them with goodness.

They deserve to be thanked for this, as no other government is able to carry out such efforts, yet they are doing it—and all praise is due to Allah. Soldiers are stationed throughout the area, along with those in authority. May Allah reward them with good. And praise be to Allah, some wear official uniforms while others do not, in order to observe the condition of the people better. This is a blessing from Allah upon these rulers.

I mentioned some of these events in my book *Ilḥād al-Khumaynī fī Arḍ al-Ḥaramayn*, referring to the turmoil that Ḥajj pilgrims experienced in the past. Al-Ḥākim Bi-Amrillāh al-ʿUbaydī, the Bāṭinī, sent one of his slaves to the Kaʿbah, where he struck the Black Stone with a mace. He then stood beside it, killing anyone who tried to stop or seize him, while shouting, "No Muḥammad and no ʿAlī!"—until two men from Yemen managed to kill him.

So, as I said previously, it is obligatory upon each Muslim in every Islamic land to support this government, because Allah says in His Noble Book,

﴿ وَتَعَاوَنُوا۟ عَلَى ٱلْبِرِّ وَٱلتَّقْوَىٰ ۖ وَلَا تَعَاوَنُوا۟ عَلَى ٱلْإِثْمِ وَٱلْعُدْوَٰنِ ۚ ﴿٢﴾ ﴾

> "And help one another in deeds of righteousness and *taqwa*, and do not help one another in deeds of sin and transgression" [*al-Māʾidah* 5:2].

And the Prophet (ﷺ) has said, "The believer to another believer is like a building—each part strengthens the other," agreed upon, on the authority of Abū Mūsá.[36] Also, the Messenger (ﷺ) said, "The example of the believers in their mutual love, compassion, and mercy is like a single body: when one part suffers, the rest of the body responds with fever and sleeplessness."[37]

Another of their virtues is honoring the scholars, something their father, ʿAbd al-ʿAzīz, strongly advised them to uphold. They hold the scholars in high regard and treat them with great respect. However, some corrupt scholars speak against the Saudi government and may even declare them disbelievers. So, it is necessary to distinguish among the people of knowledge: those who uphold the correct creed of Tawḥīd deserve respect, while those who follow deviant beliefs or partisan ideologies (*ḥizbiyyah*) do not. These *ḥizbis*, my brothers, are dangerous. They are preparing themselves to seize power whenever the opportunity arises. It is essential not to support them in any of their falsehood, except to advise and win them over, if there is hope that they will repent.

Honoring the scholars is one of their virtues and a benefit to their country and their father, ʿAbd al-ʿAzīz, who instructed them to uphold this practice.

May Allah reward them with goodness. They received us kindly, treated us with generosity, and fulfilled all our needs regarding my treatment and more. May Allah reward them for all they have done for us. I ask Allah to bless them, protect their country, keep them firm, and grant them righteous and sincere advisors. Allah says,

﴿ يَٰٓأَيُّهَا ٱلَّذِينَ ءَامَنُواْ لَا تَتَّخِذُواْ بِطَانَةً مِّن دُونِكُمۡ لَا يَأۡلُونَكُمۡ خَبَالًا وَدُّواْ مَا عَنِتُّمۡ قَدۡ بَدَتِ ٱلۡبَغۡضَآءُ مِنۡ أَفۡوَٰهِهِمۡ وَمَا تُخۡفِي صُدُورُهُمۡ أَكۡبَرُۚ ١١٨ ﴾

"O you who believe! Take not as your advisors those outside of your Religion, since they will not fail to do their best to corrupt you. They desire to harm you severely. Hatred has already appeared

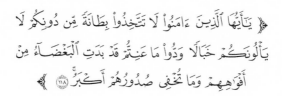

> from their mouths, but what their breasts conceal is far worse. Indeed, We have made plain to you the *Ayāt*, if you understand" [*Āli 'Imrān* 3:118].

So, may Allah grant them sincere advisors and protect them from evil companions. Indeed, the Messenger (صَلَّى ٱللَّهُ عَلَيْهِ وَسَلَّمَ) says, "The example of the good companion and the bad companion is like that of the seller of musk and the blacksmith. As for the seller of musk, you may buy from him, he may give you some, or you will simply enjoy a pleasant scent from him. As for the blacksmith, he may burn your clothes, or you will be exposed to a foul odor."[38]

However, the point here is not to continue listing the *āyāt* and *aḥādīth* about the harms of bad companions or the virtues of good ones. Rather, we advise them to keep the company of righteous companions, those who seek good for them and for the Muslim lands because this country is considered a stronghold and a place of refuge for Muslims around the world. And I praise Allah, for they have indeed welcomed many travelers from various countries. So, we praise Allah. *Wallah al-musta'ān.*

Finally, I repeat: the reason for this statement is that I believe I must speak the truth. This is an obligation. By Allah, no material gain or person has pushed me to say this. Praise be to Allah. I am not someone who is deceived by words. I judge by actions. I have seen good and praiseworthy actions here, and that is what moves me. May Allah reward them with goodness. *Wallah al-musta'ān.*"[39]

APPENDIX IV

THE FINAL DAYS

THE NOBLE BROTHER Abū Ziyād Khālid Baqays relates, "I recall the night of the *Shaykh's* trip to Germany. I was with him in the VIP section of the airport in Jeddah. We sat for a few minutes, then the *Shaykh* asked me, "Where is your car?" I told him that it was near the door of the lounge. "Let us go there and rest," he said. I took the *Shaykh* by the hand and walked him to the car. He stretched out in the back seat and began reciting some lines of poetry, and he was in wonderful spirits. An employee came to inform us that the flight was about to take off. The *Shaykh* exited the vehicle, repeating some verses of poetry. I bid him farewell at the exit of the lounge.

As my brothers know, the *Shaykh* first went to America for treatment, then returned to Saudi Arabia and Yemen, planning to go back to America to complete the treatment. However, he was denied a return visa, so the next option was Germany. Here, I'd like to share an anecdote I heard from the *Shaykh*. He said, "A female ambassador from America came to Yemen and wanted to visit Dammāj. When they arrived, I said, 'Let her go to the women's section, and the men to the men's section.' She was not pleased with that. She got angry and swore that no *Salafī* would ever enter America. But later, I traveled there myself." The *Shaykh* then laughed and said, "It is upon her to make expiation for her vow."

When the *Shaykh* arrived in Germany, they found his condition so serious that there was nothing they could do for him. They advised him to return to his homeland. Realizing what this meant, the *Shaykh* wrote his last will and testament while in the hospital in Germany.

After several days, Ṣāliḥ b. Qāyid informed me of the *Shaykh's* arrival, so I went to the airport to meet them. However, when I arrived, they informed me that *Shaykh* was very ill and was taken to the hospital in an ambulance.

When I arrived at the hospital with one of the brothers, I asked about the *Shaykh* and was told he was in the emergency department. When I entered his room, I found him alone. As soon as he saw me and my companion, he called out loudly, "Ḥayya Allah hādhihi al-wujūh (May Allah preserve these faces)," repeating it while bursting into tears. It felt as though, upon seeing us, the *Shaykh* felt he had truly returned to Saudi. I took his hand and kissed it and kissed his forehead. He was overjoyed to see us. At that moment, one of his companions entered, and the *Shaykh* said, "I've burdened you with travel and kept you away from your family." Then the brothers left, and I remained with him, holding his hand and speaking with him. Suddenly, he slipped into a coma.

I would visit him daily at the hospital while he was in a coma. On one occasion, I was there holding his hand and reading, when someone behind me gave *salāms*. I turned and saw it was our *Shaykh*, Rabīʿ ibn Hādī. When he saw *Shaykh* Muqbil, he began to cry, and everyone in the room was moved to tears. He made *duʿāʾ* for the *Shaykh*, then quietly left.

The Shaykh's Death

A GROUP OF US were in the Shaykh's room, gathered around his bed while he remained in a coma. Then, suddenly, he clenched his teeth, his eyes fixed upward, and he passed away.

I want to take this opportunity to warn against what some have circulated, that during the *Shaykh's* burial, while we were in the graveyard, he raised his forefinger, uttered the testimony of faith, and smiled. All of this is false, and the *Shaykh* has no need for such stories. His deeds, Allah willing, are a true testimony to a good end. Perhaps some mistook the clenching of his teeth as a smile—but this is incorrect. I was standing directly in front of him and bear witness to what I saw. May Allah have mercy on him.[40]

APPENDIX V

THIS IS OUR CALL AND OUR CREED

[1]: We believe in Allāh and His Names and Attributes, as they were mentioned in the Book of Allāh and in the Sunnah of the Messenger of Allāh (صَلَّى ٱللَّهُ عَلَيْهِ وَسَلَّمَ), without *taḥrīf* (distortion), nor *ta'wīl* (figurative interpretation), nor *tamthīl* (making a likeness), nor *tashbīh* (resemblance), nor *ta'ṭīl* (denial).

[2]: We believe that calling upon the dead and seeking aid from them, and similarly with the living, in that which no one besides Allāh is capable of, is *Shirk* with Allāh. Likewise, believing that charms and amulets can bring about benefit along with Allāh, or without Allāh is *Shirk*, and carrying them without that belief is superstition.

[3]: We take from the apparent meaning the Book and Sunnah, and we do not interpret anything except with an evidence from the Book and Sunnah requiring interpretation.

[4]: We believe that the Believers will see their Lord in the Hereafter, without inquiry into the modality. And we believe in the Intercession (*al-Shafā'ah*) and in the people of *Tawḥīd* being taken out of the Fire.

[5]: We love the Companions (رَضِيَ ٱللَّهُ عَنْهُمْ) of the Messenger of Allāh (صَلَّى ٱللَّهُ عَلَيْهِ وَسَلَّمَ), and we hate those who speak against them. We believe that to speak ill of them is to speak ill of the Religion, because they are the ones who conveyed it to us. And we love the Family of the Prophet (صَلَّى ٱللَّهُ عَلَيْهِ وَسَلَّمَ) with love that is permitted by the *Sharī'ah.*

[6]: We love the people of *Ḥadīth* and all of the *Salaf* of the *Ummah* from *Ahl al-Sunnah.*

[7]: We despise *'ilm al-kalām* (theological rhetoric, and we view it to be from amongst the greatest reasons for the division in the *Ummah.*

[8]: We do not accept anything from the books of the *fiqh* (jurisprudence), nor from the books of the *tafsīr* (exegesis), nor from the ancient stories, nor from the *Sīrah* (biography) of the Prophet (صَلَّى ٱللَّهُ عَلَيْهِ وَسَلَّمَ), except that which has been confirmed from Allāh or from His Messenger (صَلَّى ٱللَّهُ عَلَيْهِ وَسَلَّمَ). We do not mean that we have rejected them, nor do we claim that we are not in need of them. Rather, we benefit from the discoveries of our Scholars and the jurists and other than them. However, we do not accept a ruling, except with an authentic proof.

[9]: We do not write in our books, teach in our lessons, or deliver sermons with anything except the Qur'ān and authentic, reliable ḥadīth. We strongly dislike what is found in many books and speeches that contain false stories and weak or fabricated *aḥādīth.*

[10]: We do not declare any Muslim a disbeliever because of a sin, except for Shirk with Allah, abandonment of the prayer, or clear apostasy. We seek refuge with Allah from that..

[11]: We believe that the *Qur'ān* is the Speech of Allāh; it is not created.

[12]: We hold co-operation with any Muslim upon the truth to be obligatory and we declare ourselves free in front of Allāh from the calls of *al-Jāhiliyyah* (pre-Islāmic times of ignorance).

[13]: We do not deem it correct to revolt against the Muslim rulers as long as they are Muslims, nor do we feel that revolutions bring about rectification. Rather, they corrupt the society.

[14]: We hold that this multiplicity of present day parties is a reason of the division of the Muslims and their weakness.

[15]: We hold that the *da'wah* (call) of the *Ikhwān al-Muslimīn* is not an upright and righteous *da'wah* that brings about the rectification of the society. Indeed, their *da'wah* is political, not religious. It is also a *da'wah* of innovation, because it is a call to making unknown allegiance and *da'wah* of *fitnah* (trial, tribulation) founded upon innovation, and all of it is built upon innovation.

[16]: We advise the brothers who work amongst them to abandon them, until nothing of their time is afforded to that which does not benefit Islām and the Muslims. And it is upon the Muslim that his priority be to Allāh in aiding Islām and the Muslims upon the hand of any Muslim under any *Jamā'ah*.

[17]: We restrict our understanding of the Book of Allāh and of the Sunnah of the Messenger of Allāh (صَلَّىٰ ٱللَّهُ عَلَيْهِ وَسَلَّمَ) to the understanding of the *Salaf* of the *Ummah* from the Scholars of *ḥadīth*, not the blind-followers of their individuals. And we know that there are those who claim *Salafiyyah*, yet *Salafiyyah* is free from them, since they bring to society that which Allāh has prohibited.

[18]: We believe that politics is a part of the Religion, and those who attempt to separate the Religion from politics are only attempting to destroy the Religion and to spread chaos. Likewise, what has been spread in some of the Islāmic countries that, 'The Religion is for Allāh, but the state is for the people,' is a call of *jāhiliyyah*. Rather, everything must be for Allāh.

[19]: We believe there will be no honor or victory for the Muslims until they return to the Book of Allāh and to the Sunnah of the Messenger of Allāh (ﷺ).

[20]: We hate the present day parties: the apostate Communist party, and the apostate *Ba'thī* party, and the apostate *Nāṣirī*, and the apostate Socialist party, and the apostate *Rāfiḍī* party. And we believe that all of the people are divided into two parties: the party of Allāh, and they are those who establish the pillars of Islām and the pillars of *īmān* (faith). And there is the part of *Shayṭān*, and they are those who wage war against the *Sharī'ah* of Allāh.

[21]: We oppose those who divide the Religion up into trivialities and important issues. And we know that this is a destructive *da'wah*.

[22]: We oppose those who belittle the knowledge of the Sunnah and say that this is not the time for it. Likewise, we oppose those who belittle acting upon the Sunnah of the Messenger of Allāh (ﷺ).

[23]: We hold that the most important affairs must be given precedence over others. So it is obligatory upon the Muslims that they give importance to *'aqīdah* (creed), then to thwart the efforts of the Communists and the *Ba'th* party.

So this cannot occur, except by holding fast to the Book and the Sunnah.

[24]: We hold that no *Jamāʿah* has the ability of facing the enemies, whether it be the *Rāfiḍī*, or the *Shīʿite*, or the *Ṣūfī*, or the *Sunnī*; up until they have true brotherhood and unity upon this *ʿaqīdah*.

[25]: We oppose those who are arrogant and claim that the callers to Allāh are *Wahhābiyyah* agents. And we know that their filthy intention is that they wish to place an obstruction between the common-folk and the people of knowledge.

[26]: Our *daʿwah* and our *ʿaqīdah* are more beloved to us than our own selves, our wealth and our offspring. So we are not prepared to part with it for gold, nor silver. We say this so that no one may have hope of buying out our *daʿwah*, nor should anyone think that it is possible for them to purchase it from us for *dīnār*, nor *dirham*. Since the politicians already know this about us, they have despaired or buying it from us with granted positions or wealth.

[27]: We love the governments in accordance to what they have of goodness, and we hate them for what they have of evil. And we do not permit revolting against them, except if we have seen clear disbelief from them about which we have a proof from Allāh, with the condition that we are capable of that, and that there not be any civil strife between the Muslims and their opponents. Since the rulers portray those who revolt against them as spies causing corruption. And thereupon, other conditions come in, refer to our other books.

[28]: We accept direction and advice from wherever it comes and we know that we are students of knowledge, we are correct sometimes and we are incorrect at other times. We are ignorant at times and knowledgeable at times.

[29]: We love the present-day Scholars of the Sunnah and hope to benefit from them and regret the passing away of many of them.

[30]: We do not accept a *fatwá*, except from the Book of Allāh and the Sunnah of the Messenger of Allāh (صَلَّىٱللَّهُعَلَيۡهِوَسَلَّمَ).

[31]: We oppose those who visit graves and other than them from amongst those who allege heresy in praise.

[32]: We oppose the calls of *jāhiliyyah*, such as nationalism and Arab-nationalism. We oppose them and we name them calls of *jāhiliyyah* and we hold that they are reasons for the downfall of the Muslims.

[33]: We are awaiting the reviver that Allāh revives this Religion with. Abū Dāwud (d.257H) - رَحِمَهُٱللَّهُ - related in his *Sunan* from Abū Hurayrah (رَضِيَٱللَّهُعَنۡهُ), from the Prophet (صَلَّىٱللَّهُعَلَيۡهِوَسَلَّمَ) who said, "Indeed, Allāh send at the head of every one hundred years a reviver for this *Ummah* who revives its Religion."

[34]: We firmly believe in the misguidance of the one who rejects the *aḥādīth* pertaining to the *Mahdī*, the *Dajjāl* (anti-Christ) and the descent of ʿĪsá Ibn Maryam (عَلَيۡهِٱلصَّلَاةُوَٱلسَّلَامُ). And we do not mean the *Mahdī* of *Rāfiḍah*. Rather, we mean the leader from the Family of the Prophet (صَلَّىٱللَّهُعَلَيۡهِوَسَلَّمَ), from the people of the Sunnah filling up the earth with justice and fairness, just as it was filled with oppression and injustice before. And we say that he is from *Ahl al-Sunnah*, because cursing the noble Companions is not from justice.

[35]: These are glimpses into our *ʿaqīdah* and our *daʿwah*. And mentioning them with their proofs would lengthen the book. Indeed, I have mentioned their proofs in *al-Makhraj min al-Fitnah*. So if one has any objection to this, then we are prepared to accept advice if it is truthful, and to refute it if it is erroneous, and to avoid it if it is stubborn rejection. And Allāh knows best.

So let it be known that this has not fully covered our *daʿwah* and our *ʿaqīdah*, since our *daʿwah* is from the Book and the Sunnah, to the Book and the Sunnah, and our *ʿaqīdah* is likewise. And Allāh is sufficient for us, and He is the best of those who are trusted. And there is no might, nor power, except with Allāh.[41]

APPENDIX VI

ADVICE TO THE STUDENT OF KNOWLEDGE

Our *Shaykh* was asked about how a person should seek knowledge, follow the right path, and remain patient throughout the journey. He answered:

All praise is due to Allah, Lord of the worlds. May peace and blessings be upon our Prophet Muḥammad (صَلَّى ٱللَّهُ عَلَيْهِ وَسَلَّمَ), and upon his family and all his companions. I bear witness that nothing has the right to be worshipped besides Him, and I bear witness that Muḥammad is His servant and Messenger.

To proceed:

The path to seeking knowledge is the same path that the righteous predecessors followed. They would begin by memorizing the Qur'an. After memorizing the Qur'an, they studied Arabic to learn proper articulation. Then they would begin listening to the ḥadīth. This is what one should begin with.

The Prophet (صَلَّى ٱللَّهُ عَلَيْهِ وَسَلَّمَ) encouraged his *ummah* to memorize the Qur'an. *Imām* Muslim narrated in his *Ṣaḥīḥ* from 'Uqbah ibn 'Āmir who said: "The Messenger of Allah (صَلَّى ٱللَّهُ عَلَيْهِ وَسَلَّمَ) once said to his companions, 'Which of you would like to go out in the morning to Buṭḥān or to al-

ʿAqīq and come back with two large, hump-backed she-camels without committing sin or severing family ties?' They said, 'All of us would love that, O Messenger of Allah.' He said, 'Then for one of you to go to the masjid and learn a single verse is better for him than a camel; and learning two verses is better than two camels; and three or four verses are better than three or four camels.'"

Such is the Sunnah of the Messenger of Allah (صَلَّى ٱللَّهُ عَلَيْهِ وَسَلَّمَ). It is authentically reported from Zayd ibn Thābit that the Prophet (صَلَّى ٱللَّهُ عَلَيْهِ وَسَلَّمَ) said, "May Allah brighten the face of a person who hears my words, understands them, and then conveys them just as he heard them."

"May Allah brighten the face" is a supplication that his face be made radiant and beautiful, full of light and pleasantness.

The knowledge that many Muslims have turned away from is one of the main reasons for their distance, their division, and their decline. Allah says,

﴿ يَرْفَعِ ٱللَّهُ ٱلَّذِينَ ءَامَنُوا۟ مِنكُمْ وَٱلَّذِينَ أُوتُوا۟ ٱلْعِلْمَ دَرَجَٰتٍ ﴾

"Allah will raise those among you who believe and those who have been given knowledge in degrees." [*al-Mujādilah*: 11]

In *Ṣaḥīḥ Muslim*, it is narrated from ʿUmar that the Prophet (ﷺ) said, "Indeed, Allah raises some people through this Book and lowers others by it."

This is the knowledge that many Muslims—and many of the children of Muslims—have turned away from. Instead, they have devoted themselves to worldly sciences. Yet Allah says about such people,

﴿ فَأَعْرِضْ عَن مَّن تَوَلَّىٰ عَن ذِكْرِنَا وَلَمْ يُرِدْ إِلَّا ٱلْحَيَوٰةَ ٱلدُّنْيَا ذَٰلِكَ مَبْلَغُهُم مِّنَ ٱلْعِلْمِ ﴾

"So turn away from whoever turns away from Our reminder and desires nothing but the life of this world. That is the extent of their knowledge." [*al-Najm*: 29–30]

And He says,

﴿ يَعْلَمُونَ ظَٰهِرًا مِّنَ ٱلْحَيَوٰةِ ٱلدُّنْيَا وَهُمْ عَنِ ٱلْءَاخِرَةِ هُمْ غَٰفِلُونَ ﴾

"They know only what is apparent of the worldly life, but they are heedless of the Hereafter." [*al-Rūm*: 7]

This heedlessness occurred because people turned to worldly sciences and abandoned the Book of Allah and the Sunnah of the Messenger of Allah (ﷺ). You find a student who can name the streets of Ṣanʿāʾ, or the streets of Alexandria, or the streets of Baghdad, but if you ask him about a verse from the Book of Allah—where it is and in which *sūrah*—you will find him unaware. If you ask him about a ḥadīth of the Messenger of Allah (ﷺ), you'll find him empty-handed.

This is not how our righteous predecessors were. *Imām* Mālik said, "Nothing will rectify the latter part of this *ummah* except what rectified its first part." And *Imām* Mālik spoke the truth. May Allah have mercy on him. You will find that the Sunni—whether he is in the land of the two sacred mosques, or in Najd, or in Egypt, or in Yemen, or in Sudan, or in any other land—you will find that his speech and the speech of his brother in another country are the same, and that his creed and his brother's creed do not differ.

Someone often comes to me and says, "We heard words like yours in such-and-such a place—from a common person." They think that students of knowledge bring something new. But the methodology of *Ahl al-Sunnah* in all Muslim lands is one: Allah said, the Messenger of Allah (ﷺ) said. This is how our righteous predecessors were.

When disagreements arise, the Prophet (ﷺ) advised us to return to his Sunnah. He said, as in the ḥadīth of al-ʿIrbāḍ ibn Sāriyah, "Whoever among you lives after me will see much disagreement. So hold fast to my Sunnah and the Sunnah of the rightly guided caliphs after me. Cling to it with your molar teeth."

The Sunnah of the Messenger of Allah (ﷺ) is a protection from misguidance. It is a safeguard from division. The Prophet (صَلَّى ٱللَّٰهُ عَلَيْهِ وَسَلَّمَ) commanded us to hold to it and clarified that whoever does not cling to the Sunnah is ruined.

Imām Aḥmad narrated in his *Musnad* from ʿAbd Allāh ibn ʿAmr ibn al-ʿĀṣ that the Prophet (صَلَّى ٱللَّٰهُ عَلَيْهِ وَسَلَّمَ) said, "Every action begins with enthusiasm, and that enthusiasm is followed by a time of fatigue. Whoever remains upon my Sunnah during that fatigue is rightly guided, and whoever turns to something else is ruined."

Also in the *Musnad* of Aḥmad, from Jābir and Kaʿb ibn ʿUjrah, with similar wording, the Prophet (صَلَّى ٱللَّٰهُ عَلَيْهِ وَسَلَّمَ) said to Kaʿb ibn ʿUjrah, "O Kaʿb ibn ʿUjrah, may Allah protect you from the rule of foolish leaders." Someone asked, "O Messenger of Allah, what is the rule of foolish leaders?" He said, "Leaders who will come after me, who do not follow my Sunnah and do not follow my guidance. Whoever believes their lies and supports them in their oppression is not from me, and I am not from him, and he will not come to me at the *Ḥawḍ*. But whoever does not believe their lies and does not help them in their wrongdoing, then he is from me, and I am from him, and he will come to me at the *Ḥawḍ*"—or words to that effect.

In the ḥadīth of Ḥudhayfah, the Prophet (صَلَّى ٱللَّٰهُ عَلَيْهِ وَسَلَّمَ) mentioned *dakhan*, and it was said, "What is it, O Messenger of Allah?" He said, "A people who do not follow my Sunnah and do not follow my guidance."

So abandoning the Sunnah of Allah's Messenger (صَلَّى ٱللَّهُ عَلَيْهِ وَسَلَّمَ) is considered misguidance. And we have seen the confusion and chaos among those who have turned away from it. For example, the Muslim Brotherhood here in Yemen began demonstrating and calling for fighting under the banner of Ṣaddām, like stray sheep with no shepherd.

As for the student of knowledge, we advise him: if he finds someone who can teach him the Sunnah, then that is what we seek. But if he cannot find someone, then he should be eager to obtain the books of Sunnah and read whatever he can. And if he is able to travel in search of knowledge, then traveling is prescribed. In fact, it is Sunnah.

Ahl al-Sunnah are the majority in the Muslim world, but regrettably, because of their division, neglect, and failure to support one another, they have become the weakest group. To Allah alone we complain.

Indeed, the Sunnah of the Messenger of Allah (صَلَّى ٱللَّهُ عَلَيْهِ وَسَلَّمَ) is not only a protection from misguidance, deviation, and destruction but also a source of honor for you, O Muslim. And Allah is the One whose help is sought.

APPENDIX VII

THE SHAYKH'S METHOD IN STUDY AND RESEARCH

When asked how he managed his time and conducted research for his works, the *Shaykh* answered:

My current routine is as follows: after the Fajr prayer, I review the research papers my brothers intend to publish. A little before sunrise, I go to a quiet place and jog briefly to refresh myself. Shortly after sunrise, we read from *Al-Ṣaḥīḥ al-Musnad mimma laysa fī al-Ṣaḥīḥayn*. Then we head to the library to research until the call to Ẓuhr prayer. After Ẓuhr, we study *Tafsīr Ibn Kathīr* and some dictation or handwriting practice.

After the Ẓuhr prayer and lunch, a midday nap is essential. If I don not nap, I cannot teach effectively. So I rest briefly until ʿAṣr, then head to the masjid. After that, there is a lesson in *Ṣaḥīḥ al-Bukhārī*, followed by a class for some of our brothers in *Ibn ʿAqīl*. After that lesson, there's about an hour of rest until sunset, then *wudhu*, then back to the masjid.

After the Maghrib prayer, there is a lesson in *Ṣaḥīḥ Muslim*, and after 'Ishā', a class in *al-Sunnah* by 'Abd Allāh ibn Aḥmad ibn Ḥanbal.

As for the research, I am working on *al-Mustadrak* by al-Ḥākim and close to finishing it. I have been tracing the hadiths that al-Ḥākim graded as authentic, in which there is some criticism or where he erred in saying, "Authentic according to the conditions of the two *Shaykhs*" or "according to the conditions of Muslim." I am tracking these instances and consider them mistakes on the part of al-Ḥākim, not on the part of al-Dhahabī. May Allah have mercy on him.

I am also working on *Aḥādīth Mu'allalah Ẓāhiruhā al-Ṣiḥḥah* (Hadiths with hidden defects that outwardly appear sound). After a few days, Allah willing, I will return to working on *al-Ṣaḥīḥ al-Musnad mimma laysa fī al-Ṣaḥīḥayn*, once I complete the current project, *in shā' Allāh*.

In any case, time these days is tight due to the large number of students. I am not satisfied with how much time I have for research. In the early days, I only had a few brothers with me, so most of my time was spent on research, and by the grace of Allah, much good came from that.

I advise my brothers—students of knowledge—to study the lives of ʿAbd Allāh ibn al-Mubārak, *Imām* Aḥmad, *Imām* al-Bukhārī, and *Imām* Muslim, and others who followed their path among the scholars of hadith, so they can learn how to manage their time. I am unsatisfied with my efforts or progress, but what cannot be achieved in full should not be abandoned entirely. And praise be to Allah. Much good has still come from it.[1]

[1] *Ghārat al-Ashritah* (1/472–473)

NOTES

[1] One of the oldest and largest tribes in Yemen; the name derives from their forefather Bakīl b. Hamdān.

[2] The capital city of the *Saʿdah* Governorate in north-western Yemen

[3] A village in the *Saʿdah* Governorate

[4] Located in *al-Ṣafra*, a district of the *Saʿdah* Governorate

[5] Lieutenant-Colonel Ibrāhīm al-Ḥamdī was the leader of a military *coup d'état* in Yemen that overthrew the regime of President ʿAbd al-Raḥmān al-Iryānī on June 13, 1974. After the revolt, al-Ḥamdī was President of the Military Command Council that governed the country. He was assassinated on October 11, 1977.

[6] Also known as "*Imām Hādi* Mosque." The *masjid* is located in the Saʿdah Governorate and was built around 897 CE. It was named after Yaḥyá b. al-Ḥusayn who was nicknamed "*al-Hādī ilá al-Ḥaqq*" (Guide to the truth) by the *Zaydī* branch of the *Shiʿites*. He was one of the founders of the *Zaydī* state.

[7] Entitled *Al-ʿAqd al-Thamīn fī Tārīkh al-Balad al-Amīn* by Taqī al-Dīn Muḥammad b. Aḥmad al-Ḥusnī al-Fāsī al-Makkī; this book contains the biographies of the narrators, scholars, rulers, callers to pray, et al who lived in Makkah.

[8] Entitled *al-Īḍāḥ ʿalá al-Miṣbāḥ* by Aḥmad b. Yaḥyá Ḥābis al-Ṣaʿdī

[9] *Matn al-Azhār fī Fiqh al-Aʾimmah al-Aṭhār* by Aḥmad b. Yaḥyá al-Murtaḍá, an *imām* of the *Zaydī* sect in Yemen

[10] A treatise of Arabic grammar and inflection, written by Abū ʿAbd Allah b. Dāwud, also known by Ibn Ajurrūm. He was a scholar of *Fiqh* and Arabic grammar. He died in 723 *Hijrī.*

[11] A treatise of Arabic grammar and inflection, written by Jamāl al-Dīn Abū Muḥammad ʿAbd Allah b. Hishām al-Anṣārī, from the *imāms* of the Arabic grammarians. He died in the year 761 *Hijrī.*

[12] A civil war in Northern Yemen fought between royalist supporters of the Mutawakkilite Kingdom and the supporters of the Yemen Arab Republic. The war began in 1962 with a *coup d'état* led by ʿAbd Allah al-Sallāl and ended eight years later in 1980 with a republican victory after dethroning King Muḥammad al-Badr.

[13] *Shaykh* ʿAbd al-ʿAzīz b. ʿAbd Allah b. Muḥammad b. ʿAbd al-Azīz al-Subayyil, from the *Ḥanbalī* scholars of Najd. He was born in the area of Qasīm in 1321 *Hijrī* and died on the 21st of *Ṣafr* 1412 *Hijrī.*

[14] A book of Arabic grammar, inflection, and morphology, authored by Bahā' al-Dīn ʿAbd Allah b. ʿAqīl al-Hamdānī, al-Miṣrī. The book is an explanation of *Alfiyyah Ibn Mālik.*

[15] Collected by Muslim in his *Ṣaḥīḥ* (no. 2699), on the authority of Abū Hurayrah.

[16] See *Ṣaḥīḥ al-Jāmiʾ* (no. 3572) of *Shaykh* al-Albānī.

[17] Compiled by Muḥammad Fu'ād ʿAbd al-Bāqī in which he collects the narrations that are agreed upon by the two *Imāms*, al-Bukhārī and Muslim, in their *Ṣaḥīḥayn*. The book contains a total of two-thousand and six (2,006) Prophetic traditions.

[18] Juhaymān b. Muḥammad b. Sayf al-ʿUtaybī, a *Kharijite* insurgent who on November 20, 1979, led hundreds of dissidents in a siege of the *Ḥaram* in Makkah. After more than two weeks, Saudi Special Forces took back the *masjid* and ended the siege. On January 9, 1980, Juhaymān was publicly executed in Makkah.

[19] *Shaykh* Muqbil was asked: "Who is a *Wahhābī*? Have they in fact changed the Religion and come with a new way?"
He answered: "As for [for the term] *Wahhabism*, it is an ascription from the plots of the adversaries of Islam. The call of *Shaykh* Muḥammad ibn ʿAbd al-Wahhāb was the call to pure Islam, and the opponents of Islam hate to see such a pure call. *Shaykh* Muḥammad ibn ʿAbd al-Wahhāb and his students committed themselves to following the Book of Allah and the Sunnah of the Prophet ... At that time, some people were worshipping Zayd ibn al-Khaṭṭāb, others were slaughtering in the name of date palms and believed in them. Many had fallen into innovation and superstition. Then, praise be to Allah, Muḥammad ibn ʿAbd al-Wahhāb stood against these practices, supported by the family of Saʿūd. It should be known that we, as callers to Allah, do not accept being called *Wahhābī*, as we do not blindly follow Muḥammad b. ʿAbd al-Wahhāb, and if we were to blindly follow, we would have blindly followed Abū Bakr or ʿUmar or ʿUthmān or ʿAlī." [*Ijābah al-Sāi'il* (p. 52)]

[20] Rabīʾ Al-Madkhalī, *Tadhkīr al-Nābihīn* (Cairo: *Dār al-Minhāj*, 1429 AH/2008 CE), pp. 390-391.

[21] Ibid 397

[22] Rabī' Al-Madkhalī, *Naṣīhatuhu ilá Ahl al-Yemen*; see: http://www.sahab.net/forums/index.php?showtopic=19199
[23] Al-Albānī, *Silsilah Hudá wa al-Nūr* (no. 851)
[24] Ibn Bāz, *Faḍl Ṭalab al-'Ilm* recording
[25] Al-Wādi'ī, *Rithá Shaykhiná Ibn Bāz* (p. 16)
[26] See: http://www.sahab.net/forums/index.php?showtopic=53985
[27] See: http://www.ajurry.com/vb/showthread.php?t=20363
[28] http://www.sahab.net/forums/index.php?showtopic=60121
[29] Muqbil al-Wādi'ī, *Al-Ṣaḥīḥ al-Musnad min Asbāb al-Nuzūl (*San'ā: *Maktabah San'ā al-Athariyyah*, 1425 *Hijrī*/2004 CE), p. 9.
[30] Muqbil Al-Wādi'ī, *Al-Shafā'ah* (San'ā: *Dār al-Athar San'ā*, 1420 AH/1999 CE), p. 1.
[31] Muqbil al-Wādi'ī, *Al-Jāmi' al-Ṣaḥīḥ fī al-Qadr* (San'ā: *Dār al-Athar San'ā*, 1427 AH/2006 CE), p. 10.
[32] Muqbil al-Wādi'ī, *Al-Ṣaḥīḥ al-Musnad min Dalā'il al-Nubuwwah* (Cairo: *Dār al-Ḥaramayn*, 1423 AH/2002 CE), p. 7.
[33] Muqbil al-Wādi'ī, *Rudūd Ahl al-'Ilm alá al-Ṭā'inīna fī Ḥadīth al-Siḥr* (San'ā: *Dār al-Athar San'ā* 1420 AH/1999 CE), pp. 3,4.
[34] He states, "Certainly, one of the greatest calamities to befall the Muslims is the division among the callers to Allah. Indeed, the opponents of Islam are determined to divide them, and worse still, they actively seek to pit them against one another.

If only the callers to Allah would reflect and return to the history of their *Salaf*, they would see that although they differed on some subsidiary issues, this did not lead them to attack one another. They had different understandings of certain matters, such as the Prophet's statement, "Whoever believes in Allah and the Last Day, let him not pray al-ʿAsr until he reaches Banū Qurayẓah." Some took the ḥadīth literally and delayed their prayer until they arrived. Others understood it as an instruction to hurry, but when they feared the time for ʿAsr would end, they prayed along the way. The Prophet did not criticize either group.

What is even greater is that the Prophet said the *mujtahid* who strives to reach a ruling and makes a mistake still receives a reward. He said, "If a judge makes a ruling and is correct, he earns two rewards, and if he is mistaken, he earns one."

The *Salaf* differed in matters for which there was more than one text, like their differing over the various wordings of the *Tashahhud.* One choosing one wording, another choosing a different one. Yet, they never found fault in one another for doing so.

The differing that the *Salaf* rejected was *al-Taḍād* (opposition), when a person rejects an authentic *ḥadīth* without explanation.

The *Salaf* did not divide into groups and schisms, each group taking an ignorant leader who misguides others. Instead, they were one *Ummah*, unifying and separating for the Sake of Allah, just as their Lord has directed them in His Statement, "Indeed, your *Walī* is none but Allah, His Messenger, and the believers—those who perform the prayers, give the *Zakāt*, and they are the *Raki'ūn* (those who bow down to Allah in prayer)" [*al-Mā'idah* 5:55].

Certainly, we do not find the differing of worldly people a strange thing, but what breaks the heart is the differing of the callers to Allah, fulfilling their adversaries' desire to see them divided.

We do not call on any group to leave off their opinions for the opinions of others. Rather, we say: let each group leave off their opinions and refer back to the Book of Allah and the Sunnah of the Messenger of Allah. As Allah said, "And in whatsoever you differ, the decision thereof is with Allah" [*al-Shūrá* 42:10].

And His statement: "O you who believe, obey Allah and His Messenger and those in authority over you. And if you differ in anything, refer it back to Allah and His Messenger, if you believe in Allah and the Last Day. That is better and more suitable for final determination" [*al-Nisá* 4:59].

Indeed, I am aware that a number of the followers of the groups only desire the truth, and if they understood that this division was not permissible in the Religion, they would have abandoned their blind, fanatical leadership.

He says later: "Certainly, this division and partisanship has weakened the Muslims, and we have all witnessed this. Rather, I swear by Allah that we are fearful that this partisanship will end up as *al-Ṭāghūtiyyah* if some of the partisans unite and divide solely for the sake of their group, and call only for its sake." [See *al-Makhraj min al-*

Fitnah, Sanʿā: *Maktabah al-Sanʿa al-Athariyyah*, 1422 AH/2002 CE, pp. 5-6, and 7.]

35 Collected by al-Bukhārī in his *Ṣaḥīḥ* (no. 439) and Muslim in his *Ṣaḥīḥ* (no. 533), from the *ḥadīth* of ʿUthmān b. ʿAffān.

36 Collected by al-Bukhārī in his *Ṣaḥīḥ* (no. 467) and Muslim in his *Ṣaḥīḥ* (no. 2585), from the *ḥadīth* of Abū Mūsá al-Ashʿarī.

37 Collected by al-Bukhārī in his *Ṣaḥīḥ* (no. 5665) and Muslim in his *Ṣaḥīḥ* (no. 2586), from the *ḥadīth* of al-Nuʾmān b. Bashīr.

38 Collected by Abū Dāwud in his *Sunan* (no. 4829), on authority of Anas b. Mālik. It has been authenticated by *Shaykh* al-Albānī in *Silsilah al-Ṣaḥīḥah* (no. 3214).

39 Muqbil al-Wādiʿī, *Mushāhdātī fī al-Mamlakah al-ʿArabiyyah al-Saʿudiyyah*, (Sanʿā: *Dār al-Athar Sanʿā*, 1426 AH2005 CE), pp. 9-25.

40 See: http://www.sahab.net/forums/index.php?showtopic=139667

41 Taken from *Tarjamah Abī ʿAbd al-Raḥmān Muqbil b. Hādī al-Wādiʿī* (p. 135-142), slightly adapted. It was translated by Maaz Qureshi.

Made in United States
North Haven, CT
19 April 2025

68107359R00050